Viking
INVADERS
AND SETTLERS

Tony D. Triggs

Wayland

Invaders and Settlers

Norman Invaders and Settlers

Roman Invaders and Settlers

Saxon Invaders and Settlers

Viking Invaders and Settlers

Series Editor: James Kerr

Designer: Loraine Hayes

Consultant: Mark Gardiner BA FSA MIFA Deputy
Director, Field Archaeology Unit (Institute of
Archaeology, London).

First published in 1992 by Wayland (Publishers) Limited,
61 Western Road, Hove, East Sussex, BN3 1JD

British Library Cataloguing in Publication Data
Triggs, Tony D.
  Viking Invaders and Settlers. –
  (Invaders & settlers series)
  I. Title II. Series
  948

ISBN 0 7502 0536 9

Typeset by Dorchester Typesetting Group Limited
Printed in Italy by Rotolito Lombarda S.p.A., Milan
Bound in Belgium by Casterman S.A.

Opposite:
Top:	A Viking carving of a ship.
Middle:	A page from the Lindisfarne Gospels.
Bottom:	A soapstone bowl.

Cover:
Extreme top:	Viking lucky charms.
Top left:	A ceremonial axe.
Top middle:	A 'horn of plenty'.
Top right:	A Runestone.
Bottom left:	A Viking ship.
Bottom right:	The main towns and cities of Viking Britain.
Back:	The Lindisfarne Stone.

CONTENTS

All words that appear in **bold** in the text are defined in the glossary.

The Vikings arrive

*Never before has such terror appeared in Britain as we are now suffering from a **pagan** race. No one ever thought that such an attack could be made from the sea. But now the church of St. Cuthbert is splashed with the priests' blood and robbed of all its ornaments. It is the holiest place in Britain, and yet these pagans have made it their hunting ground.*

A man called Alcuin wrote these angry words in a letter to the King of Northumbria (northern England and southern Scotland) in AD 793. A group of Vikings had raided and robbed a **monastery** on an island called Lindisfarne, just off the coast of northeast England. Viking means 'pirate', and

ABOVE *A Viking carving of a ship.*

ABOVE *The remains of a Viking ship in a museum in Norway.*

LEFT *Some of the monks on Lindisfarne spent their time making beautiful copies of parts of the Bible. This is a page from the Lindisfarne Gospels.*

the Vikings soon made similar raids on many parts of England and Scotland. No one who lived near the sea felt safe.

The people who lived in England and southern Scotland were known as the Saxons. They lived in villages where they grew their own food and made clothes from their sheep's wool. A few Saxons had grown rich by selling cloth, and they hid their money and treasure to stop the Vikings stealing it. However, they could not hide their land, and the Vikings began to drive the Saxons out of their homes and live on their farms.

LEFT *This tombstone was found on Lindisfarne. It shows a party of Viking warriors.*

Britain in Saxon times

[Map labels: Jarlshof, SCOTLAND, Lindisfarne, NORTHUMBRIA, IRELAND, MERCIA, WALES, EAST ANGLIA, CORNWALL, WESSEX, KENT]

complained about the Vikings after being attacked. They made them sound like evil, snarling savages, but perhaps there were good things about them too. They were certainly clever. At Jarlshof in the Shetland Islands they built a farm that had its own bathhouse. Water was thrown over heated stones, giving the Vikings a steamy bath. This shows that some of the Vikings liked to be clean and comfortable, and a Saxon writer said that they often combed their hair, bathed and changed their linen underclothes. But deciding what is true and false can be very hard. Another writer said that some of the Vikings 'had as many fleas as donkeys do'!

As you find out more about the Vikings you can try to make up your own mind about them.

The people who lived in northern Scotland were called Picts and the Vikings treated them in a similar way. At first the Vikings attacked small islands off the coasts of England, Scotland and Wales. Then they began to arrive with armies, and they threatened people who lived on the mainland. The Saxons tried to save their land (and their lives) by paying the Vikings to stay away, but sometimes the Vikings took the money and attacked just the same. For example, in AD 865 the Vikings took money from the Saxons in Kent but then 'stole away inland by night and wrecked all eastern Kent.'

The Vikings attacked Ireland and other countries, as well as Britain, and according to an Irish writer:
Everyone, in every house, suffered at the hands of these evil, violent, pagan people.

It is not surprising that people

The Viking site at Jarlshof in the Shetland Islands.

The Vikings' homeland

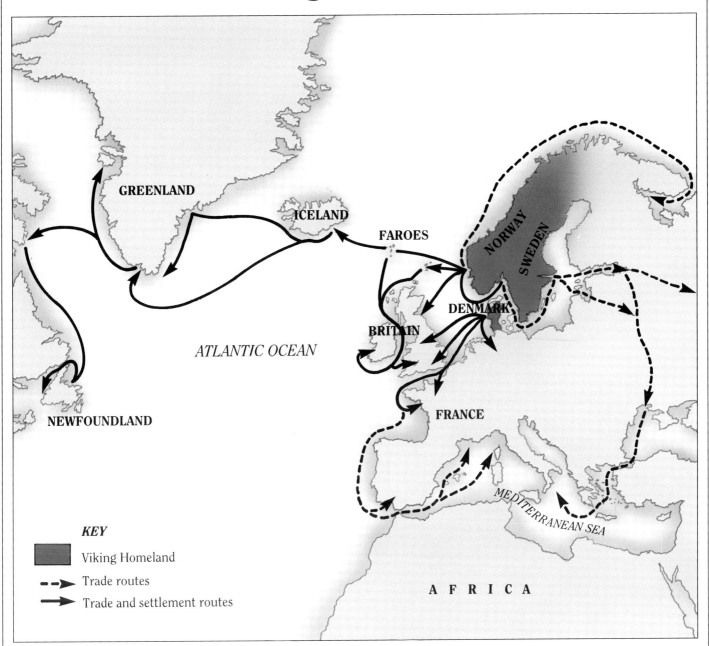

GREENLAND

ICELAND

FAROES

NORWAY

SWEDEN

DENMARK

BRITAIN

ATLANTIC OCEAN

NEWFOUNDLAND

FRANCE

MEDITERRANEAN SEA

AFRICA

KEY

Viking Homeland

- - -> Trade routes

——> Trade and settlement routes

The Vikings came from Scandinavia (Norway, Sweden and Denmark). They were very skilful at building ships and rowing and sailing across the seas. To reach Britain they had to cross the North Sea, which was often stormy even in summer. They also sailed much further west, where European people had never been before. Some of these Viking explorers drowned, but others reached Iceland, Greenland and Newfoundland (which is now part of Canada). They built themselves homes and started farming in these places.

Most of Scandinavia was covered in forests and mountains, and Viking hunters killed reindeer and other animals there. They ate the animals' meat and made themselves clothes from the skins. When they wanted to build new houses or boats they cut down some trees and used the wood.

The Vikings had plenty of furs, wood and things made of metal to sell to people in other countries. Viking merchants had boats which carried about twenty people. They loaded the boats with goods then they sailed up the rivers of central Europe. Sometimes they even carried their boats across land to get to rivers in Asia. They exchanged their goods for silk, silver and spice from the East and wine from Germany. The Vikings in Scandinavia also traded with Vikings who had settled abroad. For example, they made stone bowls and sold them to Vikings in Iceland and Britain.

ABOVE *A Viking merchant used these scales to check the weight of his customers' coins.*

A soapstone bowl.

The Vikings' raid on Lindisfarne came at the end of one of their first long voyages. No one knows why they started travelling to foreign countries as traders and settlers. Perhaps they had only just learned how to make themselves suitable boats. Or perhaps the number of Vikings in Scandinavia was growing and they had to find new land – or else starve.

Hnefetafl

The Vikings played a game called *hnefetafl*. They used a board with 121 squares, like the one in the picture. Why not play the game yourself? First you will need to copy the board on to paper or card. (Choose your own designs for the decorated squares, but try to give them a Viking look.) Then make or find some playing pieces. You will need twenty-four light-coloured pieces (called 'white') and thirteen dark-coloured pieces (called 'black'). One of the black pieces needs to be larger than all the rest. This is the king.

To start the game, put the white pieces on the patterned squares at the edge of the board and put the king in the middle with the black pieces round it.

Black and white take turns to play. The pieces move forwards, backwards or sideways. You can move the pieces as many squares as you like, as long as there is nothing in their way. If they sandwich an enemy piece, the enemy piece is removed from the board.

The black king tries to reach one of the corners; the white pieces try to take the black king or get in its way, but they cannot go on to the three squares in each corner. It's a tricky game but the Vikings loved to play it during winter evenings.

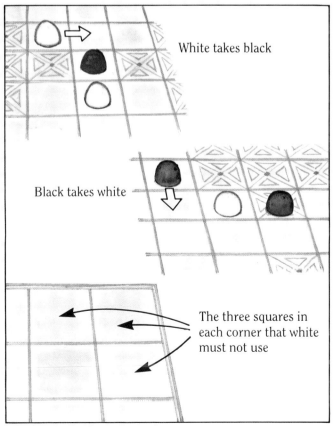

White takes black

Black takes white

The three squares in each corner that white must not use

Viking gods

According to a Viking writer called Snorri Sturluson the Vikings' main god was Odin:

Odin is the highest and oldest of the gods; he rules all things and however powerful the other gods are, they all serve him just as if they were children and he was their father . . . Because of this, Odin is called the All-father. He is also called the Father of the Killed because men who die in battle go to Valhalla – the Hall of Dead Heroes – to be with him.

The Vikings believed that Odin had female warriors to help him. According to legends, these women, called *Valkyries*, rode into battle and picked out the men who had died most bravely. They

A Viking with his weapons. This carving is on a stone cross in Yorkshire.

took them to *Valhalla*, where they served them with **mead** and **ale** from the skulls of the men's victims.

Ordinary people did not expect to go to *Valhalla* but they did expect to have another life when they died. They thought they would still want their favourite possessions; this is why brooches, weapons, board games and dice are often found in Vikings' graves. Women believed that the goddess Freyjr would welcome them into the land of the dead.

Thor, like Odin, was a very important Viking god. Thor's name was like the Viking word for thunder (*thunor*), and the Vikings believed that thunder was the sound of Thor's chariot going through the skies.

A Norwegian museum has this display of a Viking buried with all his weapons.

The Vikings in Scandinavia sometimes worshipped their gods in temples. There was a very fine temple at Uppsala in Sweden, and the Vikings killed animals and hung them in a tree near the temple to please the gods. In Britain the Vikings probably prayed in the open air near very old trees or at springs where water bubbled out of the ground.

We cannot be sure that the Vikings ever sacrificed people to please their gods, but at Buckquoy in the Orkney Islands some Vikings buried a new-born baby in the floor of a farmhouse. They had cut the baby up, and some people think they had killed and buried it when they finished the building. They probably thought this would please the gods and bring them good luck or protect their roof from stormy winds.

A smith's mould and some of the lucky charms he could make with it. One or two of the charms show the hammer Thor was said to use.

This horn-shaped container from someone's grave was full of the person's most precious possessions.

The Danelaw

By AD 878 Vikings from Denmark (known as Danes) had conquered most of England, but the Saxons still ruled the south and west. The southern counties (known as Wessex) had their own king, whose name was Alfred. When the Danes invaded Alfred's kingdom in AD 878, he gathered an army and defeated them at a place called Edington. They fled on their horses, but according to a Saxon writer: *Alfred chased them right to their fort, and he and his men surrounded it for fourteen nights. Then the Danes gave Alfred **hostages**, and they swore great **oaths** that they would go from his kingdom. They also promised that their king [Guthrum] would become a **Christian**.*

After three weeks Guthrum came to Alfred with thirty of his leading men, and Alfred had him **baptized** as a Christian. He stayed with the king for twelve days, and they gave each other all sorts of gifts. Alfred and Guthrum agreed that the Danes would keep the parts of England

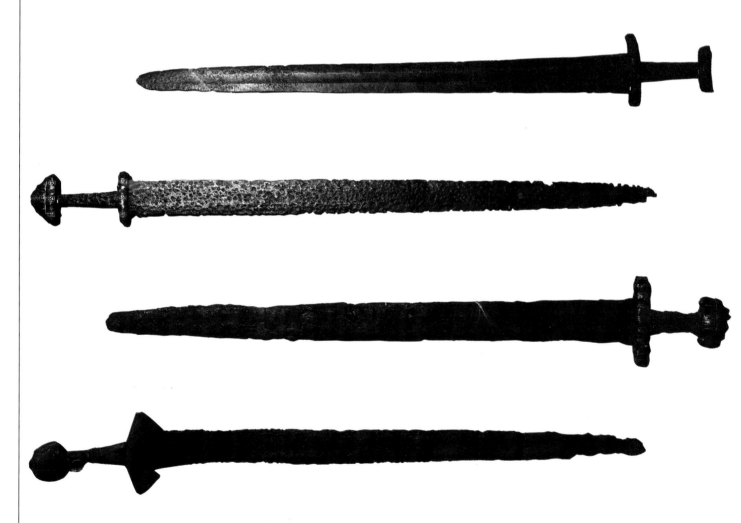

ABOVE and RIGHT *Viking swords.*

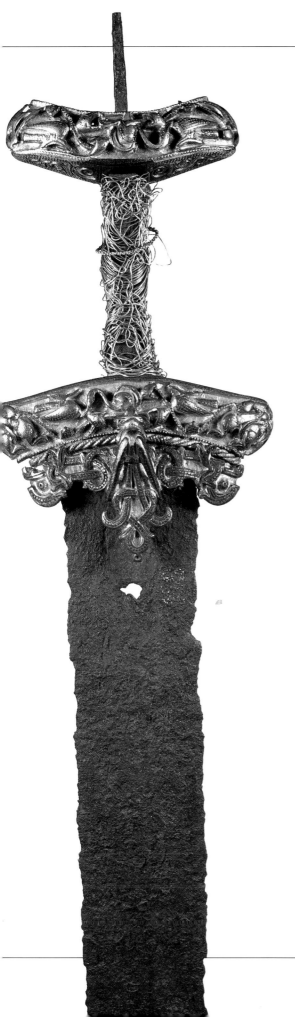

they had already conquered, and people began to call this area the **Danelaw**. The Danes were already farming there, but because it was such a large area they did not need to drive the Saxons off their land. There was room for everyone, and the Danes built new villages and started farming new plots of land.

The Danish word for village was '*by*', and we can pick out places where the Danes settled because the names have 'by' at the end. Derby is a good example; its name is made from the Danish words for 'deer' and 'village'.

The head of a special Viking axe. People think it was made to show a king or chieftain's importance.

The Saxons and Danes had different languages, but they could usually understand each other. Sometimes they even married each other, and in the end the languages got mixed up. This mixture has turned into modern English, so we still use words that the Danes and other Vikings used. The word 'law' is a good example of this, and in 'by-law' – a law for a single town or village – both words are Viking (the first is the one that we find at the end of place names like Derby).

King Alfred, who led a Saxon army against the Danes.

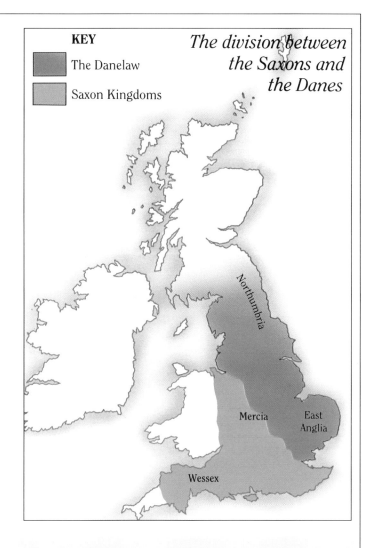

The division between the Saxons and the Danes

KEY
The Danelaw
Saxon Kingdoms

Northumbria

Mercia

East Anglia

Wessex

A place name experiment

Put a large outline map of England, Wales and southern Scotland on your wall. Then think of some place names that end with 'by'. Find out where the places are and mark their positions with flags or labels pinned on to the map. If there are lots of examples in your area, just mark one or two.

You can leave the map on the wall and add extra names as you think of them. Use maps or an atlas to check on parts of the map that don't have any examples. Try to mark twelve to twenty places on your map. What does your map tell you? How does it match what you have read in this book?

Viking towns

Viking traders lived in towns. Sometimes the towns were completely new (like Dublin in Ireland) but sometimes they were Saxon towns that the Vikings took over. They captured York in AD 866 and they turned it into one of the busiest towns in the world. It had about 2,000 houses, and a lot of the Vikings used their homes as places where they could make and sell things.

This model shows the scene outside some homes in Viking York.

The Vikings in York had two different ways of building houses. Some of the houses were like huge baskets; the walls were made by weaving bendy sticks together and fixing them on to upright posts in the soil.

The other way of building a house was to dig a large pit and line the walls with planks. The pit was so deep that the Vikings could live in it. Their heads came up to the top of the pit, but a sloping roof gave them extra room. This kind of house

*One of the sunken houses at York. **Archaeologists** have found the floor and the lowest part of the walls.*

had a door at the back and a slope or some steps leading up to the garden.

Both sorts of houses had **thatched roofs**, and floors made of soil with a ring of clay or stones in the middle. This was the fireplace; the ring stopped burning logs from rolling against the walls and setting the house or street on fire.

Making a model Viking house

Your model will show a Viking house dug into the soil, like some of the ones that were found in York.

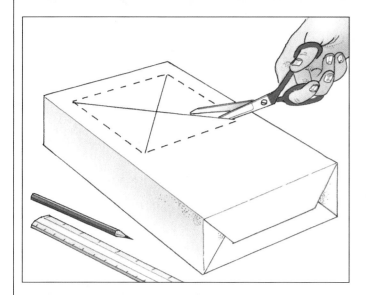

1. Take a large cereal box and draw a large square on it. The exact position isn't important, but it needs to be nearer one end than the other. Make cuts across the square in an X shape as shown.

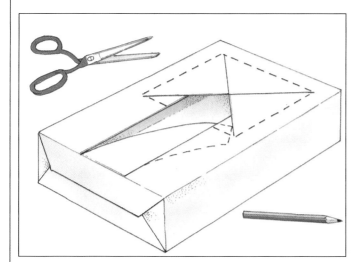

2. Make these extra cuts. They should be about 6 cm apart. You will finish up with a long 'tongue' of card that slopes down and rests on the bottom of your box. This will be the Vikings' garden path.

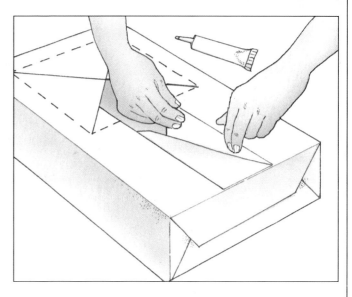

3. Glue strips of card at each side of the slope as shown.

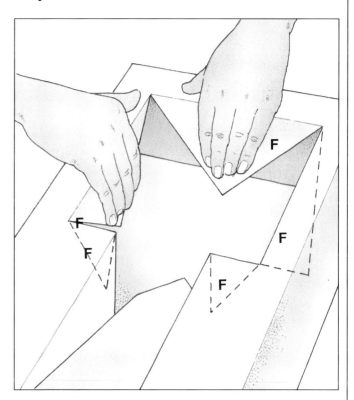

4. Fold down the five flaps marked 'F' to make a square hole.

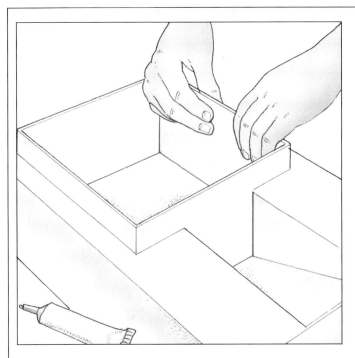

5. Take two more pieces of card and fold them so that they go all round the square hole. (Each piece should 'line' two sides of the square.) They should stick up about 2 cm.

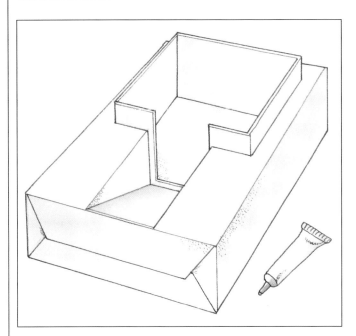

6. Cut a door as shown and then glue the pieces of card in place.

7. Add anything inside the house that will make it more realistic, such as a fireplace.

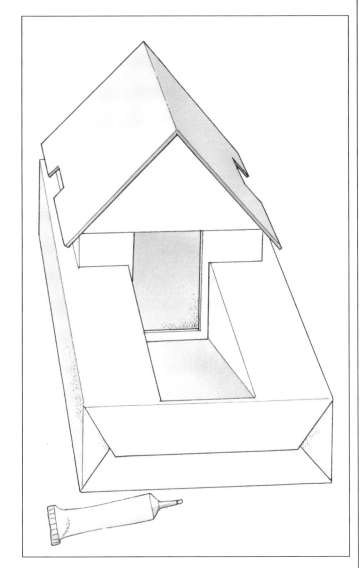

8. Take some card and fold it so that it makes a steep, sloping roof for the top of your house. Make a pair of cuts in each side as shown, and use them to 'clip' the roof into place on each side of your house, adding glue to make it more secure.

9. Fill in the triangular spaces at the front and back of your house (or leave one open so that you can see inside).

10. Paint your model and, if possible, thatch the roof with straw.

Viking crafts

Archaeologists dug up the remains of some Viking houses in York. In two of the houses they found little pots like thimbles or egg cups. There were blobs of metal on some of the pots, so the Vikings must have used them for melting metal

Living in one of the houses at York.

over their fires. The archaeologists also found pieces of stone with shapes cut into the surface. The Vikings poured the hot metal into the shapes and let it cool and harden. One of these **moulds** was for making cheap jewellery.

Viking patterns

The Vikings sometimes drew animals with long legs and bodies, and even long jaws. They made these parts so long that they could link them together in criss-cross designs called animal interlace, and sometimes they added letters called runes. Runes were used to spell out words, for decoration or for working magic.

Draw and colour your own Viking pattern, and make it look mysterious by adding some runes.

The archaeologists at York also found special moulds called dies for making silver coins. Instead of melting the silver, the Viking took a silver **disc** and placed it

Coins and a die for making them. You can also see a strip of metal which the coin-maker used for testing his dies.

The Vikings covered this stone with runes and the tangled patterns they loved so much.

ABOVE *Making bowls.*

between a pair of dies; then he hit the upper die with a hammer, and the patterns on the dies got pressed into the disc.

Some streets in northern England and Scotland still have names that the Vikings gave them. York's Coppergate got its name from a pair of Viking words that mean 'cup-makers' street'. Nearby, archaeologists have found small knobs of wood in the soil. The Vikings in Coppergate made wooden cups, and the knobs are bits of wood they removed to make the cups hollow.

Working out dates

Archaeologists handle every piece of wood with care.

Archaeologists often find coins in the soil. The patterns or words on the coins show when they were made, and this gives a clue to the date of other things that may be buried nearby.

Archaeologists can also use the rings in wood to work out dates. If you look at the stump of a tree, you can see these rings for yourself. Each ring shows how much the tree – and other trees in the area – grew in a year. If a ring is close to the previous ring, it means that the weather was cold and the trees did not grow much; if the rings are a long way apart the weather was warm and the trees grew a lot.

Archaeologists know the pattern of rings in trees that grew hundreds of years ago. When they find bits of wood from a Viking building, they can use the pattern of rings in the wood to work out the date when the tree was cut down.

Wooden objects found at York. They are resting on modern planks. Look at the planks and try to decide why they have lines instead of rings.

More clues in the soil

Archaeologists look for clues about how this pit was used.

Near some Viking houses archaeologists have found deep holes that the Vikings dug. The holes are full of soil and rubbish and the archaeologists have had to clear this out, taking care not to miss any clues about the Vikings' lives. They can usually work out why the Vikings dug each pit. Some were wells, some were toilets and some were used for storing things.

The wells and the toilets were near to each other, and filth from the toilets got into the Vikings' drinking water. This made them ill, and it explains why they often died young. Archaeologists can tell the age at which people died by examining their bones; skeletons found in Viking graveyards show that they rarely lived to be fifty.

In the Vikings' toilets, archaeologists sometimes find 'coprolites' (pieces of human dung that have turned into fossils). The coprolites often have bits of grain from the bread and porridge the Vikings ate. They also have eggs from the worms that lived in the Vikings' bodies.

Bones that the Vikings threw out into their gardens show that they also ate all sorts of meat, birds and fish. At York, archaeologists found some cows' skulls with holes in the top. Perhaps the Vikings killed them by hitting them over the head with an axe.

A Viking farm

In some ways the lives of Viking farmers and Vikings who lived in towns were similar. Men did the jobs that needed most strength, like dealing with cattle or beating metal into shape, but everyone helped with other jobs. There were no schools to go to, so children had to join in the work like everyone else. Perhaps they helped their mothers to make the family's clothes.

The Vikings made most of their clothes from sheep's wool. They started by spinning the wool into thread, then they wove it into cloth on **looms**. They coloured the cloth with dye from plants such as madder and woad. The Vikings' clothes were colourful but the designs were plain. (Cutting the cloth to make interesting shapes would have made it fray and fall apart.)

Archaeologists digging at Viking sites often find heavy clay rings like the ones in the picture below. Viking women tied them to threads on their looms to keep the threads tight. The rings are so common that some people think nearly all Viking families made their own clothes.

LEFT *Life in a Viking home.*

ABOVE *Weaving on a Viking loom.*

Sometimes archaeologists find the remains of a Viking farm. This picture is based on remains that were found at Ribblehead in North Yorkshire. Patterns of mounds and boulders on a grassy hilltop showed where the buildings had stood, and three coins gave a clue to the age. People had probably lived there in the tenth century.

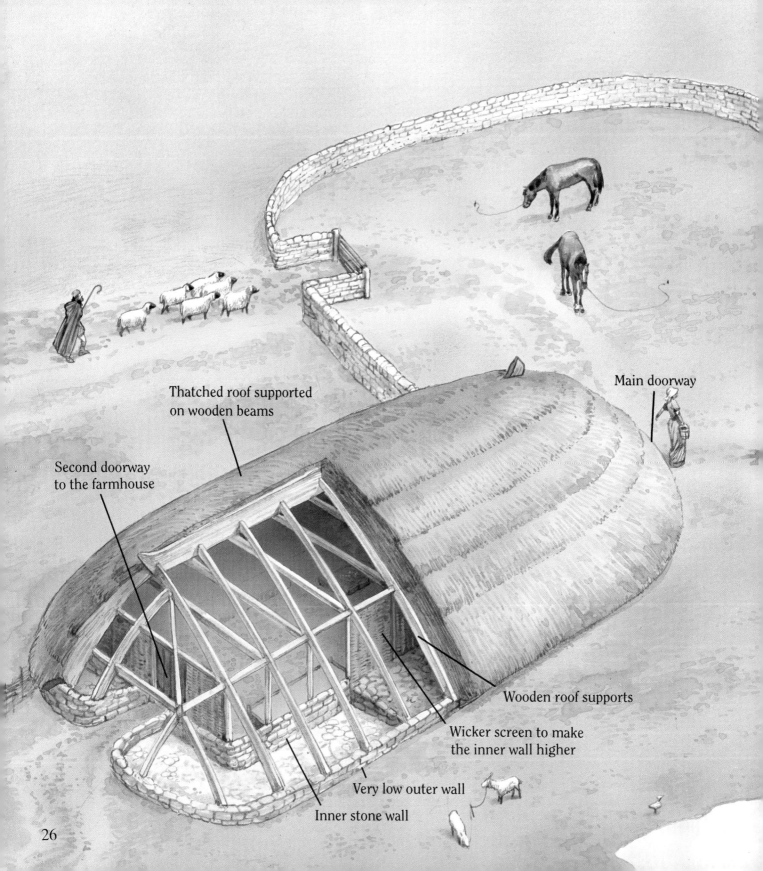

Thatched roof supported on wooden beams

Main doorway

Second doorway to the farmhouse

Wooden roof supports

Wicker screen to make the inner wall higher

Very low outer wall

Inner stone wall

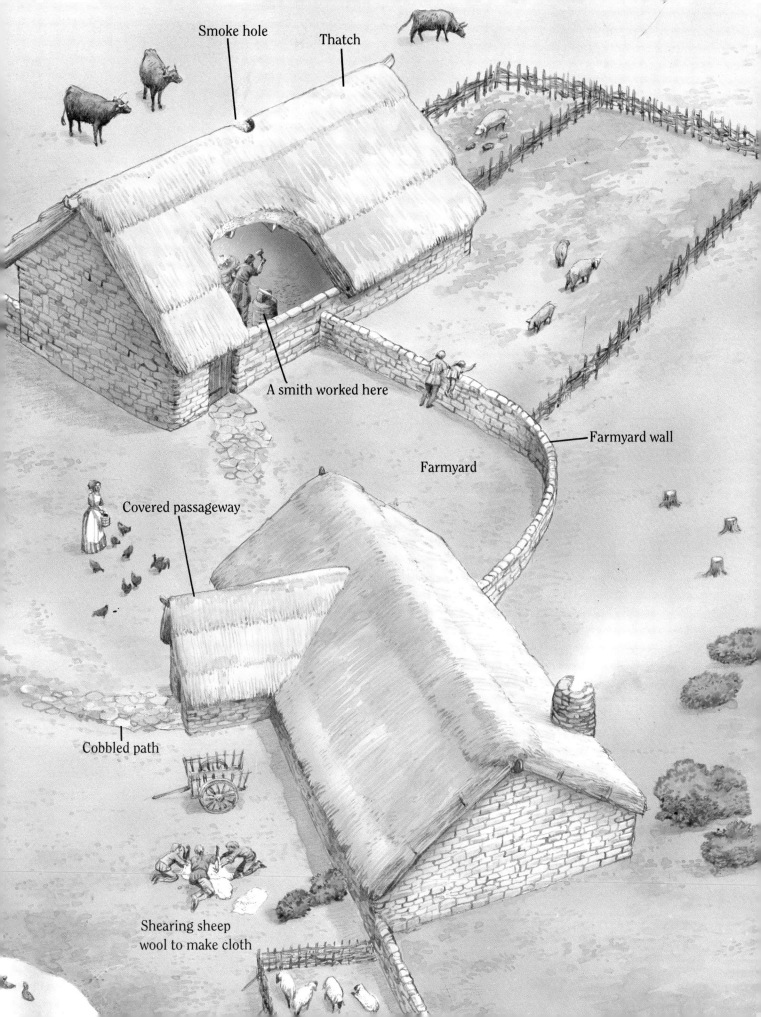

Smoke hole

Thatch

A smith worked here

Farmyard wall

Farmyard

Covered passageway

Cobbled path

Shearing sheep
wool to make cloth

The end of the story

ET VENIT AD PEVENE SÆ:

The Normans on their way to England. This picture comes from the Bayeux Tapestry.

In the eleventh **century** new groups of Vikings came from Scandinavia, and they tried to gain control of England and southern Scotland. In 1066 Harold Hardrada, the King of Norway, landed with an army in northern England. The Saxons, led by their own King Harold, beat the Norwegians, but Vikings who had settled in northern France also invaded England. These Vikings were known as Normans or Northmen (Men from the North). Their leader, Duke William, sailed across the English Channel with a fleet of ships and a well-prepared army. They defeated Harold's exhausted army in the Battle of Hastings.

The contest between the Vikings and Saxons had come to an end. The different peoples continued to mix, but some things the Vikings left have lasted right to the present day. Farmhouses in the north of England are often on sites that the Vikings chose, and the farmers stick to Viking ways of caring for sheep and making cheese. Some of the tools they use are based on Viking examples, and the farms have often kept the names that the Vikings gave them. Some of the farmers have Viking names too.

A lot of our commonest surnames go back to Viking times. Kerr and Carr are good examples; they come from the Viking word meaning 'marsh'.

Many museums have objects that the Vikings made, and churches and churchyards sometimes have the stones they carved with strange designs. In cities like York we can see the remains of Viking buildings and we can walk in modern streets which are just where the Viking ones were. In some parts of Britain we can even eat food which the Vikings invented. For example, they invented a kind of oatcake. Cooks who call them havercakes are using the Viking name as well as the Viking recipe!

Skillets like this, based on Viking originals, were used for cooking until the early twentieth century.

AD 750	
Vikings explore, raid and settle **AD 800** many of the places they can reach in their ships. They trade throughout Europe and much of Asia.	**793** Vikings destroy the monastery at Lindisfarne.
AD 850 Vikings from Norway settle in parts of north-west England and Scotland.	**865** Vikings start staying the winter in England.
	876 A Viking army marches through England and captures York.
AD 900	**878** King Alfred of Wessex defeats the Danes. They divide England between them.
	928 The Saxon king Athelstan rules England, Wales and southern Scotland.
AD 950 Saxon kings rule the whole of England.	**954** Eric Bloodaxe, the last Viking ruler of York, is driven out by the Saxons.
	978 England has a weak king called Ethelred. The Danes make new attacks.
AD 1000	**1016** After Ethelred's death, England is ruled by the Danish king Cnut and his children.
AD 1050	**1042** England is once again ruled by a Saxon, Edward the Confessor.
AD 1100	**1066** Edward is followed by Harold, another Saxon. Harold defeats Danish invaders in northern England, then Normans defeat him in the Battle of Hastings. The Norman leader, William the Conqueror, becomes King of England.

Glossary

Ale   A sort of beer.

Archaeologist   Someone who digs up and studies objects and remains from the past.

Baptize   To sprinkle or bathe a person with water as a sign that he or she has become a Christian.

Century   A period of 100 years. For example, the eleventh century is the period from the beginning of AD 1000 until the end of AD 1099.

Christian   Someone who believes in Jesus Christ.

Danelaw   The part of England ruled by the Danes.

Disc   Something round and flat, like a coin.

Hostages   People who are captured and held so that they can be used to bargain with the enemy.

Loom   A sort of frame on which people weave cloth.

Mead   A drink made from honey.

Monastery   A place where people live, pray and obey strict rules because of what they believe about God.

Mould   A solid object (usually stone) with a hollow shape in it for shaping liquid metal.

Oath   A solemn promise.

Pagans   People who believe in many gods.

Thatched roof   A roof made from straw.

Books to read

The Vikings by M Gibson (Wayland, 1987)

The Vikings by R Place (Longman, 1980)

Viking Britain by T D Triggs (Wayland, 1989)

The Viking Dig by R Hall (Bodley Head, 1984)

The Vikings: Fact and Fiction by R Place (Cambridge University Press, 1985)

A Viking Sailor by C Gibb (Wayland, 1982)

Viking Warriors by T D Triggs (Wayland, 1989)

Places to visit

Cambridge: Museum of Archaeology and Ethnology
Douglas, Isle of Man: Manx Museum and Art Gallery
Dublin: National Museum of Ireland
Edinburgh: National Museum of Antiquities of Scotland
Kirkwall, Orkney: St. Magnus Cathedral; Tankerness House Museum
London: British Museum; Museum of Mankind; *Victoria and Albert Museum

Middleton, North Yorkshire: Church of St. Andrew
Oxford: Ashmolean Museum
*Reading: Museum (Blagrave Street)
Sumburgh Head, Shetland: Jarlshof
York: Castle Museum; Jorvik Viking Centre; Yorkshire Museum

*The Bayeux Tapestry is on display at Bayeux in France, but these museums have copies. It is advisable to check in advance that the copy will be on display.

Index

Picture Acknowledgements

The publishers would like to thank the following for providing pictures used in this book: Aerofilms 6; Ancient Art and Architecture Collection 4 (bottom), 12, 14; C M Dixon cover (top right), back cover, title page, 5 (top), 10 (both), 20-21, 30, 31; Calderdale Leisure Services 29; Michael Holford 13 (left), 28; Werner Forman Archive cover (extreme top, top left, top middle, bottom left), contents page (top and bottom), 4 (top), 5 (bottom), 8 (both), 11 (both), 13 (right); York Archaeological Trust contents page (middle), 9, 15, 16, 19, 20 (left), 21 (both), 22 (both), 23, 25.

Artwork: Peter Bull 6, 7, 9, 14, 17-18; Peter Dennis 24, 26-7; Malcolm S Walker cover (bottom right).